REFLECTIONS OF INDIA

André Wagner

REFLECTIONS OF
INDIA

HANS-NIETSCH-VERLAG

Navneet Raman

VORWORT

Indien ist wie ein Spiegel, in dem sich die ganze Welt selbst erkennt. Dieses Land wirft die tiefsten Gedanken der Menschen zurück, die es bereisen und erfahren. André Wagners Reise nach Indien ist eine Reise zum eigenen Selbst. Er als Fotokünstler macht diese Reise, um zu sehen, und wird andererseits selbst durch dieses Buch sichtbar. Wie Jiddu Krishnamurti sagte: „Der Beobachter wird zum Beobachteten ..."

In der heutigen Welt, die sich wirtschaftlich in einer Krise befindet, ist es angebracht, für einen Augenblick innezuhalten und einen frischen und anderen Blick auf Indien zu werfen, das gemeinhin als eine der größten und sich am schnellsten entwickelnden Volkswirtschaften gilt, als Land der Computer und der Verbraucher.

Was Indien heute ist und was es morgen sein wird, durch die Spiritualität und die Toleranz seiner Menschen. André Wagner gibt uns die Gelegenheit, diese Facette des indischen Lebens kennenzulernen. Die ruhigen Bilder zeigen eine intensive Wirklichkeit, die vielen Besuchern entgeht, wenn sie durch ein Land eilen, das die räumliche Größe und die kulturelle Vielfalt Europas besitzt.

André Wagners „Reflections of India" ist eine Sammlung ruhiger Augenblicke inmitten des absoluten Chaos, das den indischen Alltag zu beherrschen scheint, doch es sind diese hier so wunderbar eingefangenen Momente, die uns die Stärke Indiens vor Augen führen. Frieden und Glück lassen sich nur dann im Außen wahrnehmen, wenn man sie in sich trägt. Das Wesen der fotografischen Kunst ist dadurch gekennzeichnet, dass sie nur das erfasst, was direkt vor unseren Augen liegt, die Wirklichkeit, wie sie von einem technischen Instrument gesehen wird. Es ist der Geist hinter der Kamera, der dieser Wirklichkeit eine weitere Dimension hinzufügt. André Wagners geschultes und zugleich junges und frisches Auge, das Indien empfindsam und respektvoll erkundet, ermöglicht uns den Zugang zu einem in der Tradition verwurzelten vielschichtigen Land.

Die 108 Fotografien in diesem Buch sind nicht nur ästhetisch ansprechend, sie zeigen auch das tiefe Verständnis, das André Wagner auf seinen vier Reisen mit insgesamt fünf Monaten Aufenthalt von der Kultur und Spiritualität der Indus-Ganges-Ebene gewonnen hat.

Nutzen wir die Gelegenheit, die uns „Reflections of India" bietet, um tiefer über unser Leben zu reflektieren.

Navneet Raman wurde 1975 in Benares geboren und besuchte die von Jiddu Krishnmurti gegründete *Rishi Valley*-Schule in Andhara Pradesh. Danach arbeitete er sechs Jahre lang in Neu-Delhis Finanzbranche, bevor er 2005 nach Benares zurückkehrte, um dort die *Kriti Gallery and Residency* zu eröffnen. Sie bietet die Gelegenheit, sich in einer der ältesten und kulturell bedeutendsten Städte Indiens mit Kunst zu befassen. Die dazugehörige Wohnanlage eröffnet Künstlern aus der ganzen Welt die Möglichkeit, sich von der Stadt Benares inspirieren zu lassen.

Navneet Raman

PREFACE

India is like a mirror on the world reflecting the deepest thoughts of people who go there. André Wagner's journey into India is a journey into one's own self. As a photographic artist, he is making this voyage to see and, in return, he himself is also seen through this book. As Jiddu Krishnamurti said: "The observer becomes the observed ..."

In the world today, engulfed in economic crisis, it is an appropriate moment to take a step back, sit down and look at India with fresh eyes. It is considered to be one of the largest markets and most rapidly growing economies among the fastest developing nations in the world – a land of computers and consumers.

India is what it is today and what it will be tomorrow because of the spirituality and the tolerance of its ordinary people. André Wagner gives us the opportunity to explore this facet of life in India. These quiet images of India display a stark reality that most travellers miss in their rush through this country, a country that is the size of Europe and culturally at least as diverse.

André Wagner's "Reflections of India" is a beautiful collection of tranquil moments in the utter chaos of daily life, and these moments give us deep insights into the strength of India. It is only possible to feel peace and happiness outside if you have that inside of you. Photography is an art that is quite different in that it only captures what is present in front of your eye – reality as seen by an instrument. However, it is the mind behind the camera that gives us another dimension to reality. André's well trained eye, young and fresh, explores India with sensitivity and respect, and opens doors into the ancient and complex Indian landscape.

The 108 photographs in the book are not only beautiful, they display a deep understanding of the landscape and civilization they capture. Taken in the short span of 4 trips and totalling a 5 months duration, they allow us a glimpse of the Indo-Gangetic Plain, as it is.

Navneet Raman Navneet Raman was born in 1975 in Banaras and educated at *Rishi Valley School* run by Jiddu Krishnamurti in Andhra Pradesh. After six years of working in the financial sector in Delhi, he moved back to Banaras and opened *Kriti Gallery and Residency* in 2005. *Kriti Gallery* is a space for interaction with art in one of the oldest living cities and a cultural capital of India. The Residency at *Kriti Gallery* provides an opportunity for artists from around the world to interact with the city of Banaras.

REFLECTIONS OF INDIA

SAI
MM
D KUMAR

श्री राधा
श्री राधा

खाद बीज
GOODEARTH.

दयाल गौड़
सबरजिस्ट्री
यहाँ पर
इकरारना,
लिखे जाते हैं
57155060,

ACTIVE
WEAR

श्री
राधा

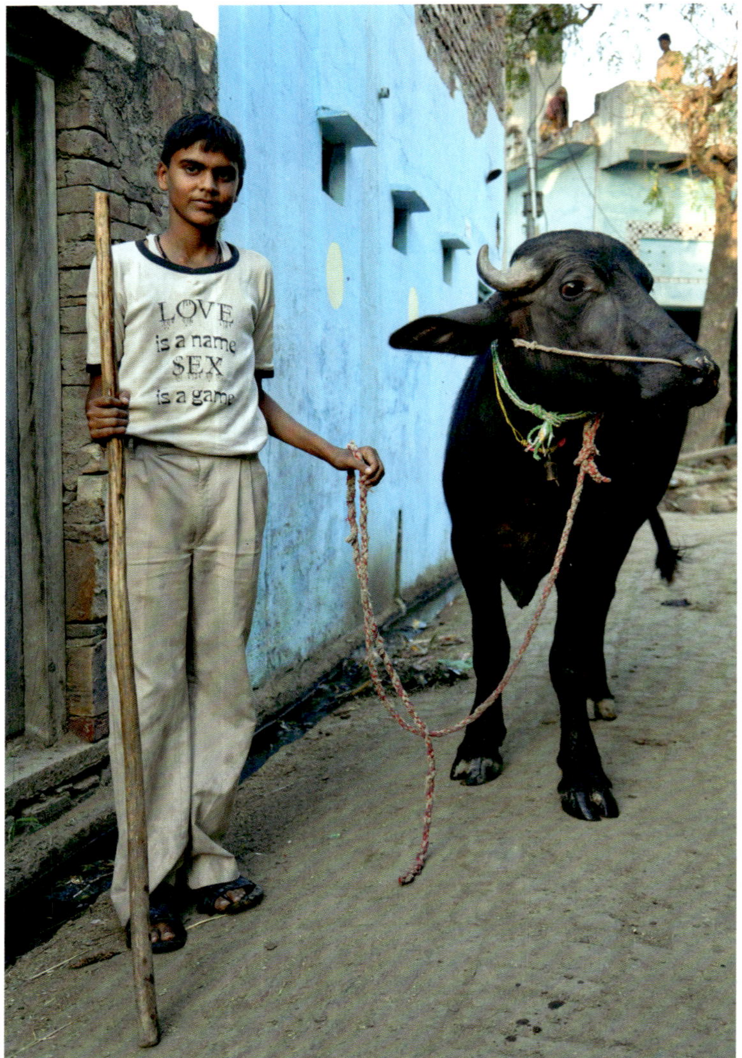
LOVE
is a name
SEX

MES BONDOO7

महाबीरराम साव पुज्यनीया बड़ी माता स्वर्गीया गुलराजी देवी
रामकली देवी की पुण्य स्मृति में सुपुत्र श्री सत्य नरायण प्रसाद साव
माता स्वर्गीया रामकली देवी की पुण्य स्मृति में सुपुत्र श्री सत्य नरायण प्रसाद साव ने श्रीजी माँ के चरणों में अर्पण किया।
पौत्र ओमप्रकाश, जय प्रकाश, विजय प्रकाश
कलकत्ता निवासी

श्री
राधा नाम
कभी न भूलें

जी हाँ
दूध

श्री
राधा
श्री

HOND

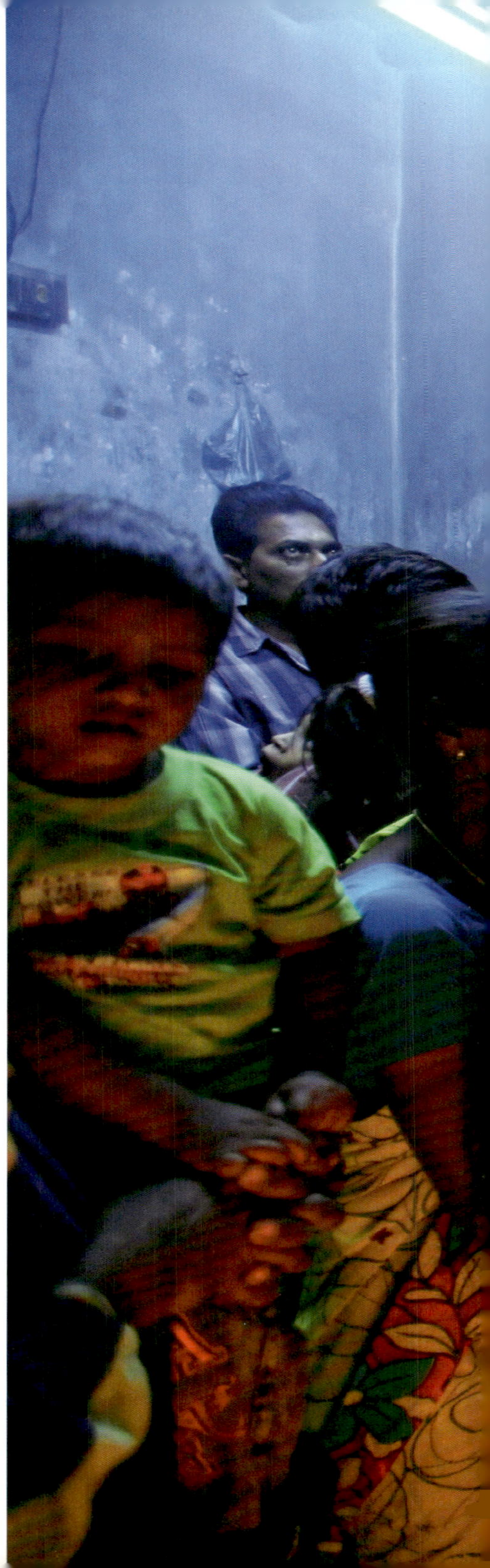

73 | 74 | 75

KISHORI
Pushpanjali
09837835522
Expert Property Advice
Shah
Properties
Sale & Purchase
* House * Flats * Villas
* Plots * Shops * Lands
9837057186
₹999
RELIANCE
Diwali Offer
Till 31st October
₹999
+5 GB usage free
RELIANCE
PEPSI
CHAITANYA KAL
SALE DEPOT SAVE YOU

SHOR
MUKUT
WALA
NANDKISHOR MUKUTWALA
NANDKISHOR MUKUTWALA
NANDKISHOR AGRAW

श्री
राधा
सदा जपिये
श्री

उप
NW
11708
विकलांगों के लिए
FOR DISABLED
19711 19712

उप
NW
03411
M.G
SNTS 6

ॐ
समाधी
स्थल
बीज मन्त्र
श्री गणेशाय नम ॥
सुदामा
कुटी
हरि

BILDTEXTE

1 Am Hauptbahnhof in Neu-Dehli
2 Riksha in Vrindavana
3 Riksha-Fahrt in Varanasi
4 Schulkinder auf dem Nachhauseweg in Vraja, Uttar Pradesh
5 Jaina auf Pilgerreise in Rajasthan
6 Straßenszene in Nandagram, Uttar Pradesh
7 Am indischen Nationalfeiertag in Navadvipa
8 In einem Dorf in der Nähe von Varshana, Uttar Pradesh
9 Eine Frau trägt Kuhdung, den sie zum Feuermachen gesammelt hat
10 Glückssymbole *(Svastika)* aus Kuhdung an einer Wand
11 Am Pilgerweg um den heiligen Berg Govardhana in der Nähe von Mathura
12 *Sankirtana* – gemeinsames Singen der heiligen Namen Gottes am Krishna-Tempel in Udupi, Karnataka
13 Kind in Varshana, Uttar Pradesh
14 Kinder mit Wasserbüffel-Kalb in Varshana, Uttar Pradesh
15 Kälber vor einer Mauer, auf der der heilige Schriftzug „Shri Radha" in Sanskrit zu lesen ist; Varshana, Uttar Pradesh
16 Hirtenjunge mit Wasserbüffel in Uttar Pradesh
17 Junger freiwilliger Helfer vor dem Lalita-Tempel-Ashram in Varshana, Uttar Pradesh
18 Jungen beim Spielen in Varshana, Uttar Pradesh
19 Eine Schulklasse wartet auf ihren Lehrer; Kolli Hills, Tamil Nadu
20 Ein Junge und sein Drachen in Pushkar, Rajasthan
21 Languren-Affen am Brahma Kund in Pushkar
22 Chili-Ernte in Tamil Nadu
23 Am Kund des Eklingeswar-Shiva-Tempels in Rajasthan
24 Blick vom Hanuman-Anjanadri-Tempel in Hampi, Karnataka
25 Ein Reisfeld wird gepflügt; Kolli Hills, Karnataka
26 Ein Reisfeld wird gepflügt; Kolli Hills, Karnataka
27 Frauen, die junge Reispflanzen setzen; Kolli Hills, Karnataka
28 Bei der Bananenernte, Karnataka
29 Das morgendliche Melken der Ziegen; Hampi, Karnataka
30 Die Affen am Berg Govardhana werden gefüttert; Uttar Pradesh
31 Männer, die Gemüse tragen; am Fluss Yamuna, Uttar Pradesh
32 Männer, die Gemüse tragen; am Fluss Yamuna, Uttar Pradesh
33 Am Keshi Ghat mit Blick auf die Yamuna; Vrindavana, Uttar Pradesh
34 Am frühen Morgen umrunden Pilger die heilige Stadt Vrindavana, Uttar Pradesh
35 Pilgerinnen, die vom heiligen Fluss Yamuna kommen; Vrindavana
36 Umkleidebereich am Keshi Ghat, einer Badestelle am Fluss Yamuna
37 Die Stufen, die zur Yamuna hinabführen
38 Gläubige auf dem Weg zum morgendlichen Darshan im Radharamana-Tempel in Vrindavana
39 Pilgernde Familie in Vrindavana, Uttar Pradesh
40 Ein Pilger fotografiert am Keshi Ghat
41 Täglicher Gang zum Yamuna-Tempel, Vrindavana
42 *Yamuna-Puja* (ein Ritual der Verehrung) mit 108 Gheelampen
43 „Shri Radha – Vergiss ihren Namen nie!"-Schriftzug in Hindi, darunter ein Krishna-Bild; Vrindavana
44 Radharani-Tempel auf dem Hügel von Varshana, Uttar Pradesh
45 Die Göttin Durga und Hanuman; Chatikara, Uttar Pradesh
46 Vishnu, der auf Garuda sitzt, rettet den Elefanten Gajendra vor dem Krokodil; links daneben der Jagannatha-Altar, Orissa
47 Ein Mönch liest vedische Texte; Mayapura, Westbengalen
48 Rituale frühmorgens im Ashram: Ein Sadhu studiert die heiligen Schriften, der andere reibt seinen Körper mit Öl ein; Varshana

CAPTIONS

1 At the main railway station in New Delhi
2 Rickshaw in Vrindavana
3 Rickshaw ride in Varanasi
4 Schoolchildren on their way home in Vraja, Uttar Pradesh
5 Jains on pilgrimage in Rajasthan
6 Street scene in Nandagram, Uttar Pradesh
7 On the Indian Republic Day in Navadvipa
8 In a village near Varshana, Uttar Pradesh
9 A woman carrying cow dung that she has collected for fuel
10 Lucky symbol (*Svastika*) consisting of cow dung on a wall
11 On pilgrimage around the holy Govardhana Hill, near Mathura
12 *Sankirtana* – congregational singing of the holy names of God at Krishna Temple in Udupi, Karnataka
13 Child in Varshana, Uttar Pradesh
14 Children with a water buffalo calf in Varshana, Uttar Pradesh
15 Calves in front of a wall on which can be read the sacred inscription "Shri Radha" in Sanskrit; Varshana, Uttar Pradesh
16 Cowherd boy with water buffalo in Uttar Pradesh
17 Young volunteer in the Lalita Temple Ashram in Varshana, Uttar Pradesh
18 Boys playing in Varshana, Uttar Pradesh
19 A school class waiting for its teacher; Kolli Hills, Tamil Nadu
20 A boy and his kite in Pushkar, Rajasthan
21 Langoor apes at Brahma Kund in Pushkar
22 Chili harvest in Tamil Nadu
23 At the Kund of the Eklingeswar Shiva Temple in Rajasthan
24 View from Hanuman Anjanadri Temple in Hampi, Karnataka
25 Ploughing a rice field; Kolli Hills, Karnataka
26 Ploughing a rice field; Kolli Hills, Karnataka
27 Women planting rice offshoots, Kolli Hills, Karnataka
28 At the banana harvest, Karnataka
29 The milking of goats in the morning; Hampi, Karnataka
30 Feeding monkeys on Govardhana Hill; Uttar Pradesh
31 Men carrying vegetables; at the Yamuna River, Uttar Pradesh
32 Men carrying vegetables; at the Yamuna River, Uttar Pradesh
33 At Keshi Ghat with view of the Yamuna River; Vrindavana, Uttar Pradesh
34 Pilgrims circumambulating the holy city of Vrindavana in the early morning; Uttar Pradesh
35 Women pilgrims, coming from the sacred Yamuna River; Vrindavana
36 Changing facility at Keshi Ghat, a bathing place on Yamuna River
37 The steps leading down to the Yamuna River
38 Devotees on their way to the morning darshan in the Radharamana Temple in Vrindavana
39 A family of pilgrims in Vrindavana, Uttar Pradesh
40 A pilgrim taking a photo at Keshi Ghat
41 Daily visit of the Yamuna Temple, Vrindavana
42 *Yamuna-Puja* (a worship ritual) with 108 ghee lamps
43 "Shri Radha – Never forget her name!"-inscription in Hindi, underneath Krishna picture; Vrindavana
44 Radharani Temple on the hillock in Varshana, Uttar Pradesh
45 The Goddess Durga and Hanuman; Chatikara, Uttar Pradesh
46 Vishnu sitting on Garuda, liberates the elephant Gajendra from the crocodile, on the left the Jagannatha-Altar, Orissa
47 Monk reading Vedic texts; Mayapura, West Bengal

Shri Sarvabhavana

INDIEN – ein Essay

Als André Wagner die Aufnahmen für dieses Buch machte, war ich zumeist anwesend. Und dabei vertraute er mir an, dass diese Bilder eine Art Linse darstellen sollen, die dem Betrachter einen direkten Zugang ermöglicht.

Für ihn ist Indien ein eigener Kosmos, der von Mystik, Kultur sowie familiären und freundschaftlichen Beziehungen voller Herzlichkeit geprägt ist, die sich auch im warmen Umgang mit Fremden wie den zufälligen Mitreisenden im Zug zeigt.

Indien wurde vom Westen erst lange nach Christoph Kolumbus' missglücktem Versuch entdeckt, der Indien auf dem Seeweg hatte erreichen wollen. Kolumbus, Vespucci, Vasco da Gama und andere Seefahrer wussten, dass es jetzt in der Ferne aufregende Länder zu entdecken gab, doch ihren königlichen Mäzenen ging es um etwas ganz anderes: Die Expeditionen sollten den Fortbestand ihrer Reiche sichern.

Als Indien ins Blickfeld anderer Kulturen rückte, hatte es bereits eine lange Geschichte hinter sich. Doch selbst nachdem man es besser kennengelernt hatte, blieb dem Rest der Welt das Wesen der indischen Seele verborgen. Die Eroberer kamen nicht, um dieses Mysterium zu entschleiern, sie hatten es auf die sagenhaften materiellen Schätze abgesehen: Gold, Edelsteine, Seide, Kräuter, Gewürze und vieles mehr. Indien wurde zum Magneten für imperialistische Kräfte und Plünderer.

Bis zum heutigen Tag nehmen Besucher Indien als ein Land der Extreme und unauflöslichen Gegensätze wahr, in dem beispielsweise Neureiche und Möchtegerne mit ihrem Reichtum protzen, unberührt von dem allgegenwärtigen Elend und Mangel. Auf der anderen Seite ist es ein Segen, dass diese Kultur jedem den Weg zu persönlicher religiöser und innerlich erfahrener Fülle eröffnet, angesichts derer die äußeren Widersprüchlichkeiten ihre Schärfe verlieren.

Und obwohl es keinem entgehen kann, dass in den Metropolen funkelnde Wolkenkratzer wie Pilze aus dem Boden schießen, in deren Schatten die Slums sich weiter ausbreiten, ist man in Indien bereit, das einfach zu tolerieren und damit zu leben.

Keine andere Kultur ist mit Indien vergleichbar, wenn es darum geht, individualistische spirituelle oder nicht-spirituelle Sichtweisen einfach ganz selbstverständlich anzunehmen. Als der heilige Thomas im 1. Jahrhundert nach Christus an der Südspitze der indischen Halbinsel landete, um die Botschaft Jesu zu verbreiten, wurde er vom damaligen König von Kerala willkommen geheißen. Die erste syrisch-christliche Kirche (die so bezeichnet wird, weil der Apostel Thomas aus Syrien stammte) wurde hier in Indien errichtet.

Als die Parsen, die feuerverehrenden Anhänger Zarathustras, von den islamischen Eroberern und Herrschern Persiens verfolgt wurden und in die Diaspora gingen, gelangten sie an die Westküste Gujarats, wo sie beim dortigen König Zuflucht und Schutz fanden und ihren ersten Feuertempel außerhalb von Persien errichteten.

Shri Sarvabhavana

INDIA – an essay

When André Wagner was taking the photographs for this book, I was usually present. And he kept confiding in me that these photographs were to be like a lens that would allow the observer direct access to India.

For him, India is a self contained world imbued with mysticism, culture and close family and friend relationships, which are also revealed in the warm interaction with strangers, encountered as passengers on trains etc.

India was discovered by Westerners much later than the first abortive attempt by Columbus to find a sea route to India. Columbus, Vespucci, Vasco D'Gama and the other seafarers knew they were on the brink of discovering some exciting far-off lands. Their royal patrons, however, had other priorities in mind: it was more about a survival strategy for their own empires.

Indian history began long before the rest of the world discovered her existence. Even when she became more widely known to other cultures, the essence of her soul remained hidden to the rest of the world. Conquerors were drawn to India, not to reveal the soul of India but to exploit her fabled treasure: gold, gems, silk, herbs and spices etc. India's superabundance in material resources was the magnet that drew imperialists and plunderers.

To the present day, India continues to be seen by foreign visitors as a land of extremes and of irreconcilable contradictions. Conspicuous wealth and consumption of the nouveau-riche and wannabees contrasts with ubiquitous squalor and poverty. On the other hand, this culture has had the good grace to allow her populace to express their religious fervour individualisticaly, mostly privately, and, in doing so, to reconcile the apparent contradictions that are the hallmarks of her vibrant culture.

The incongruity of lavish skyscrapers sprouting like mushrooms in the neighbourhoods of spawning squalid ghettos in large cities cannot go unnoticed. For better or for worse, people in India have learned to live with it.

No other culture has such an innate sense of tolerance and acceptance of individualistic spiritual and non-spiritual views as is still seen today in India. When Saint Thomas arrived in the southern tip of the Indian peninsula fifty years after Christ to preach his message, the then King of Kerala welcomed him. The first church ever to be built in the Orient, which became known as the Syrian Christian Church, St. Thomas having come from Syria, was constructed here in India.

When in Persia the Parses, fire-worshipping followers of Zarathustra, were persecuted by the conquering and proselytising Islamic rulers, the diasporas landed on the western shores of Gujarat, only to be welcomed and given shelter by the King. The first ever Fire Temple outside of Persia, the land of its origin, was built here.

With the exception of the Vedic *Sanatana Dharma*, all other world religions practice proselytisation. Followers of *Sanatana Dharma* or Hindus believe that religion is an individual and entirely personal

Außer dem vedischen *Sanatana Dharma* versuchen fast alle Religionen zu missionieren. Für die Anhänger des *Sanatana Dharma*, die Hindus also, ist Religion eine Angelegenheit, die vollkommen der Selbstbestimmung des Einzelnen unterliegt, daher ist es ihnen fremd, Nicht-Hindus bekehren zu wollen, um so „ihre verlorenen Seelen zu retten".

Darüber hinaus lehren die Veden, dass sich jeder Mensch zuerst selbst darum bemühen soll, beispielhaft und selbstlos in seinem Verhalten zu werden, bevor er andere auffordert, sich zu ändern oder zu bessern.

In Indien gibt es mehr als hundert Völker, die nach wie vor ihren alten Traditionen gemäß leben und ihre eigene Sprache sprechen. Sie wurden also nicht gewaltsam zu Hindus gemacht und entgingen so dem Schicksal zahlreicher Völker in anderen Ländern, die sich der Lebensweise der Mehrheit der Gesellschaft anpassen oder ihre Heimat verlassen mussten. Diese ethnischen Minderheiten verloren ihre Wurzeln und ihr kulturelles Erbe auf dem Opferaltar der Intoleranz von religiösen Eiferern und dünkelhaften Fanatikern.

Religiöse Freiheit und Selbstbestimmung gehören so untrennbar zur hinduistischen Ethik und zu den vedischen Schriften, dass sie nicht unterdrückt oder ausgemerzt werden können. Auch die Versuche skrupelloser, korrupter Politiker, die heute ihre Ziele mit allen Mitteln erreichen wollen, ändern nichts daran.

Das Gesetz des *Karma* – das Gesetz von Ursache und Wirkung – ist ein Pfeiler, auf dem das vedische Wissen ruht. Das Gesetz beschreibt und definiert das Wirken von Mutter Natur. Es ist komplex, weil die materielle Welt vollständig der Dualität und dem Faktor Zeit unterliegt. Das Sanskritwort *karma* bedeutet einfach „Handlungen, die entsprechende Folgen zeitigen".

Insgesamt gibt es drei verschiedene Arten von Handlungen. *Karma* sind Handlungen, die mit den Vorschriften der Schriften übereinstimmen und zeitweilig materielles Glück zum Ergebnis haben. *Vikarma* sind Handlungen, die die Gesetze der Natur verletzen und zu verschiedenen Formen von Leid führen. *Akarma* sind Handlungen, die keine materiellen Wirkungen haben, sondern zur Befreiung aus dem Kreislauf von Geburt und Tod führen. Das komplexe Wirken des *Karma*-Gesetzes ist ein unerschöpfliches Thema. Eine kurze Definition des Gesetzes lautet: Der Wechsel von Freude und Leid in einem Leben ist eine Folge der Handlungen in früheren Leben.

Die vedische *Karma*-Lehre kann daher nicht mit den fatalistischen Sichtweisen mancher anderer Kulturen gleichgesetzt werden, die von einem unausweichlichen Schicksal ausgehen.

Die Veden bieten eindeutige Unterweisungen, die einen Weg zeigen, wie das höchste Ziel des Lebens erreicht werden kann. Diese Unterweisungen werden aber nicht von Drohungen begleitet, dass derjenige ewiger Verdammnis anheimfallen wird, der nicht in der Lage oder willens ist, sie zu hören oder zu verstehen.

Falls es kein eigenständiges Streben nach Transformation im Bewusstsein und auch keinen Drang gibt, spirituelles Wissen zu erlangen, bleiben äußere Veränderungen im Verhalten – auch wenn es um religiöse oder moralische Handlungen geht – ohne nachhaltige Wirkung. Daher fordern die Veden uns auf, innere Wandlung durch hohe spirituelle Erkenntnis und spirituelle Praxis zu erreichen.

Das moderne Indien steht heute vor der Aufgabe, seine spirituelle Identität inmitten des rasanten technischen Fortschritts neu zu definieren. Die indische Regierung möchte das Wirtschaftswachstum und die Versuche hervorheben, Schandflecken wie Armut und Korruption zu beseitigen. Korruption ist allgegenwärtig in der Politik und fängt bereits bei den Ministern an und sogar Sisyphos hätte vor der Aufgabe kapituliert, anständige Politiker aus ihnen zu machen. Minister prangern lautstark Korruption und Vetternwirtschaft an und wissen gleichzeitig, dass sie nur Theater spielen, wenn sie der Welt und ihrem Volk versprechen, für Abhilfe zu sorgen.

belief. Hence the urge to convert non-Hindus with the intention of saving their "wayward and lost souls" is absolutely foreign to their religious agenda.

The Vedas teach that before anyone tries to improve the world or to convince another to transform or convert, that person must first become a better and selfless human being themself and be of exemplary behaviour.

To this day in India, more than a hundred types of aboriginal peoples live, practice their traditions and speak in their own dialect. They were not forcibly converted to Hinduism, unlike in other countries where aboriginals had to convert and to conform to mainstream society, or else to leave. These ethnic communities in foreign lands lost their heritage and traditions at the sacrificial altar of intolerance and supercilious attitudes of religious zealots and fanatics.

This respect for religious freedom is so ingrained in the Hindu ethos and in the Vedic scriptures that it can neither be suppressed nor uprooted even by the Machiavellian manipulations of unscrupulous, corrupt politicians trying to achieve their political ends. This coercion can be seen in modern India today.

The law of *Karma,* or the law of cause and effect, is one of the foundation blocks on which the edifice of Vedic knowledge stands. This law describes and defines the complex working of Mother Nature. It is complex because the material world is fully controlled by duality and the time factor. The Sanskrit word *Karma* simply means "actions, which produce concomitant results".

In all there are three types of actions: *Karma* are actions that are in consonance with scriptural injunctions and bear results in the form of material and evanescent happiness. *Vikarma* are actions that violate the laws of nature resulting in different forms of suffering, and *Akarma* are actions which do not produce any material results but which generate freedom from the continuous cycle of birth and death. The intricate functioning of the law of *Karma* is a subject of endless discussion. However, a succinct definition of this law reads that the amount of temporary joy and suffering one experiences in life are the results of one's previous actions.

Hence, we can see that the Vedic paradigm of *Karma* cannot be equated with the view of an inexorable fate prevalent in other cultures.

The Vedas offer unequivocal instructions regarding how to attain the sumuum bonum of human life. These instructions are not accompanied by threats of eternal damnation in hell if one is not in a position to, or just not interested in hearing and understanding them.

Unless there is a desire for voluntary and sincere transformation in consciousness, together with the urge not to remain in ignorance of higher, spiritual truths, any external behavioural changes, be they performances of religious rites, pious or moral acts, such transformation is not sustainable. This in mind, the Vedas exhorts us to undergo inner transformation through proper knowledge of the Absolute truth and regular practice of spiritual discipline.

Modern India is caught in the bind of technological progress on the one hand, and redefining her spiritual identity in this context, on the other. The government wants to showcase India's financial growth and its attempts to eradicate the ugliness of poverty, corruption etc. Corruption is so rampant at all levels starting with the ministers themselves, that Sisyphus himself would have given up trying to make honest leaders out of them. The ministers loudly condemn corruption and nepotism, when all the while they know in their rotten hearts that they are making a grand show of hollow promises to the world and their people.

André's lens captures the brazen deceitfulness of politicians who foolishly neglect the basic tasks of conservation, road maintenance, policing and other infrastructural necessities that provide security, cleanliness and hygienic residential facilities for the citizens.

Andrés Kamera fängt die Verlogenheit der Politiker ein, die nicht in der Lage sind, die grundlegendsten Aufgaben zu erledigen, die den Bürgern eine funktionierende Infrastruktur, Sicherheit und angemessene hygienische Standards garantieren.

Die Aufnahmen, die André machte, zeigen oft deutlich das Dilemma, in dem die Inder stecken: Sollen sie sich mit einem Leben abfinden, in dem Korruption ganz selbstverständlich dazugehört, oder sollen sie sich dagegen auflehnen? Inder akzeptieren gewöhnlich ihr *Karma*. Sie wurden dazu erzogen, familiäre Verantwortung zu tragen. Das ist die stärkste Triebfeder in ihrem Leben.

Eltern bemühen sich, so gut sie können, für ihren Nachwuchs zu sorgen. Entscheidungen, Regeln und ethische Grundsätze sind von dieser Verantwortung motiviert, und die Inder machen keinen Hehl daraus, dass die Familie für sie an erster Stelle steht. In ihren Gebeten bitten sie vor allem um Beistand für Familienmitglieder und Freunde. Das lässt sie weniger selbstbezogen und egoistisch sein.

Hindus haben keinen speziellen Wochentag, an dem sie in den Tempel gehen. Üblich ist es vielmehr, dort besondere Anlässe zu feiern, wie Jahrestage, Geburtstage, den ersten Schultag oder Arbeitstag … Im Prinzip steht in jedem Heim – und sei es noch so beengt – an einem sorgsam ausgewählten Platz ein Altar, an dem Gott täglich mit kleinen Ritualen verehrt wird.

Ich habe gesehen, dass auch kleine Schulkinder dem Altar Ehrerbietung erweisen, bevor sie aus dem Haus gehen. Und der Ladenbesitzer führt zu Beginn des Tages ein kleines Ritual vor dem Altar durch, den er in seinem Laden aufgestellt hat. Natürlich muss er zu Mitteln wie Lügen und Betrügereien greifen, um seine Waren zu verkaufen und über die Runden zu kommen – und dafür wird er den Segen der Gottheit erbitten.

In den Städten ist es üblich, dass sich Tagelöhner unter einem riesigen Banyanbaum vor einem kleinen Tempel treffen, um Gott mit ihren Gesängen zu lobpreisen, wobei sie von Trommeln und Zimbeln begleitet werden. Wenn ich mich recht entsinne, machte André eine seiner Aufnahmen von Hanuman – dem „Affengott“, wie ihn Westler gern nennen – in der Abenddämmerung, bevor das gemeinsame Singen beginnen sollte.

Bestimmte Aspekte des indischen Lebens sind Mitgliedern anderer Kulturen nur schwer zu vermitteln, da sie in sich nicht einfach zu begreifen sind. Nehmen wir die heiligen Kühe und das Kastensystem. Für Muslime oder Christen ist das Fleisch von Kühen ein bevorzugtes Nahrungsmittel, nicht jedoch für die Anhänger der Veden. Für sie ist die Kuh ein Symbol materiellen Reichtums, sie repräsentiert Lakshmi, die Gottheit der Fülle und des Wohlstands.

Rinder versorgen die Menschen in Indien mit lebensnotwendigen Dingen und verrichten viele Dienste, so tragen sie zum Beispiel Lasten. Und obwohl die Technik auch in diesem Land Einzug in die Landwirtschaft gehalten hat, mit all den negativen Begleiterscheinungen wie beispielsweise Luftverschmutzung, so bleibt hier der vom Ochsen gezogene Pflug doch das sicherste Gerät.

Kuhdung ist Brennstoff, Dünger und ein Mittel zur Sterilisation und zum Desinfizieren. Im *Ayurveda* gilt der Urin der Rinder als Heilmittel und wird seit Jahrhunderten zur Leberreinigung, bei Gallensteinen, Magenbeschwerden und vielem anderen eingesetzt. Kuhmilch liefert wichtige Nährstoffe für die Gehirnzellen.

Geklärte Butter oder Ghee ist eines der besten Speisefette. Nachdem sie mehr als zehn Jahre kühl aufbewahrt wurde, ist sie bei chronischen Hautkrankheiten ein ausgezeichnetes Heilmittel zum Einreiben. Rindsleder ist für manche Musikinstrumente, für Kleidung und Schuhe das beste Material.

Abgesehen davon sind Kuhmilch, Ghee, Rinderdung etc. seit Jahrtausenden feste Bestandteile vedischer Rituale und religiöser Zeremonien. Der Rauch, der aufsteigt, wenn Ghee als Opfergabe verbrannt wird, hat eine starke reinigende und energetisierende Wirkung.

The pictures André took often highlight the helplessness of ordinary Indians caught on the horns of a dilemma, whether to go on with life as if corruption is normal, or protest until they become hoarse against it. Ordinary Indians have an innate quality of acceptance of their *Karma*. They have been brought up to shoulder the responsibility of family. This is also the driving force.

Parents are focussed on raising their children to the best of their capacity. Decisions, moral and ethical considerations etc. are defined by this duty of family responsibility. Indians do not usually feel shy about admitting to this. Their prayers to their God are indeed solicitations for the fulfilment of wishes and desires of their family members and friends. This makes them less self-centred and egoistic.

For the Hindus there is no one day in the week reserved for a visit to the temple. Temple visits are usually intended to celebrate special occasions like anniversaries, birthdays, first day of school or work and so on. Practically every home, even an overcrowded room or flat, has often a tiny altar occupying a prominent space in the residence where God is worshipped daily with simple rituals.

I have seen that even small schoolchildren, before leaving home, offer obeisance at the altar. The shop owner will perform a short ritual at the altar he set up in his shop at the start of the day. Make no mistake, the shop owner will have to lie and cheat to sell his wares to make ends meet – he will pray for his Deity's blessings to enable him to do this.

It is quite common in cities in the evenings to see the daily wage earners, after a day's hard work, gather under a huge banyan tree in front of a tiny temple to sing together in praise of God to the accompaniment of drums and cymbals. In fact, if I remember correctly, one of André's frames of Hanuman, the monkey-god (as Westerners commonly refer to him) is in this book and was taken at dusk, when the congregational singing was about to begin there.

Certain aspects of Indian life, culture and tradition are not easy for her ordinary citizens to explain to others. These topics simply do not allow themselves to be made readily comprehensible to most people from other belief systems.

Take, for example, the holy cow, or the caste system. To Muslims or Christians beef is a favourite food, but not to the Vedic followers. The cow is a symbol of material prosperity for the Vedic followers. The cow represents Goddess Lakshmi, the Deity of abundance and opulence.

In India the cow and the bull furnish basic necessities and provide services for ordinary people. They carry burdens and although technology has replaced the natural way of farming in this country also – and not without the pernicous side effect of air pollution – ox-drawn ploughing here still remains the safest.

Cow dung is a fuel, a fertiliser and a sterilising and disinfecting agent. In *Ayurveda*, cow urine has been used for many centuries in liver dialysis, in the treatment of gall-bladder stones, general stomach ailments, and for many other complaints. Cow milk supplies important nutrients to the brain cells.

Clarified butter, or Ghee, made from cow's milk is one the best cooking fats and when kept cool for a period of ten years or more, is an excellent remedy for chronic skin diseases when applied. Cattle skins are best suited for certain percussion instruments, as they are for clothes and shoes.

Besides these material benefits, cow-milk, Ghee, cow-dung and so on have for many millenniums been indispensable ingredients in Vedic rituals and religious ceremonies. The smoke from Ghee offered as an oblation in fire has extremely strong purifying energy that can increase the number of negative ions in the atmosphere.

The caste system within the Vedic paradigm is known as the *Varnashrama* system. In truth this division in human society exists in practically all cultures in an amorphous manner. There are in all

Das Kasten-System ist in der vedischen Lehre als *Varnashrama* bekannt. Dass die menschliche Gesellschaft in verschiedene „Klassen“ unterteilt wird, findet sich in praktisch allen Kulturen auf die eine oder andere Weise. In Indien gibt es vier Kasten oder Klassen: *Brahmanas* sind die Priester, Lehrer und Intellektuellen. *Kshatriyas* sind der Adel, die Beschützer der Schwächeren in der Gesellschaft und Mitglieder der staatlichen Verwaltung. *Vaishyas* sind die Händler und Geschäftsleute und *Shudras* sind die ungelernten Arbeiter und Dienstboten.

Dieses System existiert im heutigen Indien allerdings nur noch in einer pervertierten Form. In der Bhagavad-Gita sagt Krishna zu Arjuna, dass er diese Unterteilung der Gesellschaft den Eigenschaften und Betätigungsfeldern ihrer Mitglieder entsprechend geschaffen hat. Die Qualifikationen und Aufgabenbereiche eines Menschen legten fest, zu welcher Kaste er gehörte. Nirgends in den Schriften steht, dass es einzig und allein die Geburt in eine bestimmte Familie ist, die über die Kastenzugehörigkeit entscheidet.

Wann immer ich in Indien bin, fällt mir auf, dass die Menschen dort ihren Alltag mit viel Improvisationstalent und Erfindungsreichtum bestreiten. Vergleicht man es mit westlichen Ländern, ist das vielleicht etwas einseitig und beruht sicher auf einem Überlebensinstinkt, der versucht, mit den hohen Anforderungen des Lebens in einer materiellen Welt zurechtzukommen.

Die Bevölkerung Indiens sucht in ihrem Inneren nach Frieden, sodass äußere Einflüsse nur begrenzt zugelassen werden und für geistige Unruhe sorgen können. Dies ist Teil ihrer Erziehung und der Eindrücke, die sie als Kinder bekommen haben, und erlaubt es ihnen, mehr oder weniger, geistig ausgeglichen zu bleiben.

In Europa hingegen funktionieren die öffentlichen Verkehrsmittel, die Verkehrsregelung und vieles mehr wie geschmiert. Und so erwarten die Menschen, dass alles gut und pünktlich funktioniert. Wenn es dann allerdings aus irgendwelchen Gründen nicht der Fall ist, reagieren sie sehr negativ. Kurz gesagt: Die Inder haben mehr Schwierigkeiten mit äußeren Faktoren, während die Westler eher innerlich, geistig aus dem Gleichgewicht kommen.

Shri Sarvabhavana wurde 1947 in Kalkutta geboren. Dort studierte er englische Literatur und Philosophie. 1969 brach er auf, um die Welt zu bereisen. Sein Weg führte ihn auch nach Deutschland, wo er sich in Hamburg für den Studiengang Visuelle Kommunikation einschrieb, den er 1974 mit dem Abschluss „Master of Arts“ beendete. Ein Jahr später kehrte er nach Kalkutta zurück und absolvierte dort ein weiteres Studium, und zwar in Vergleichender Religionswissenschaft und Philosophie.

Im Jahr 1981 begegnete Shri Sarvabhavana dem großen Mystiker Pujyapada Sri Himangshu Chakravartyji, der ihn als Schüler annahm und elf Jahre lang in der bengalischen *Sattvika Tantra*-Tradition unterrichtete.

Seit 1978 übersetzt Shri Sarvabhavana vedische Schriften aus dem Alt-Bengali und dem Sanskrit ins Englische. Allein bis 1996 erschienen 14 Bände dieser Werke, die zwischen 500 und 5000 Jahre alt sind und sich mit der Philosophie des *Bhakti Yoga* – in dessen Mittelpunkt die Hingabe an Gott und der persönliche Aspekt Gottes stehen – befassen.

Seit 1996 lebt Shri Sarvabhavana eine Hälfte des Jahres in Berlin, die andere in Indien. Er ist bis heute als Übersetzer tätig und seit 2012 Gastdozent für Hinduismus an der Theologischen Fakultät der Humboldt Universität in Berlin (Internationaler Masterstudiengang „Religion und Kultur“).

four castes or classes in India: *Brahmanas* are the priests, teachers and intellectuals; *Kshatriyas* are royals, protectors of the weaker section of society and administrators; *Vaishyas* are the mercantile and business community and farmers; *Shudras* are menial, unskilled labourers.

Presently in India, this system exists but only as a mere perversion of its original form. In the Bhagavad-gita, Lord Krishna tells Arjuna that he established the division of society according to one's qualities and activities. Specific qualifications and occupational engagements are prerequisites for being categorised in a particular caste. Nowhere in the scriptures is it written that birth in a particular family is the only defining factor for belonging to a caste.

For me personally, whenever I am in India I observe how people in general deal with daily affairs in a manner that seems highly innovative – sometimes too much so – in comparison to the people in western countries. Their innovativeness is certainly born out of survival instincts in the face of the increasing demands of life in the material world.

The populace in India by and large try to find a peaceful inner space where the external situations are not always allowed to intrude and disturb their mental make-up. This is part of their upbringing and the early impressions they receive as children help them acquire mental equipoise to varying degrees.

In Europe, things like public transport, maintenance and repair, traffic control and a long list of other urban services work like a well-oiled machine., People expect everything to function properly and on time. When this does not occur for some reason or other, the people's reaction is very negative. I would sum this up by saying that people in India suffer more from external disturbances and in the west more from internal, mental perturbation.

Shri Sarvabhavana was born in Calcutta in 1947. There he studied English Literature and Philosophy. In 1969 he left to travel the world. His travels led him to Germany where in Hamburg he enrolled on a course on Visual Communications from which he graduated in 1974 with a Master of Arts degree. A year later he returned to Calcutta undertook further studies and graduated in Comparative Religion and Philosophy.

In 1981 Shri Sarvabhavana encountered the great mystic Puyjapada Sri Himangshu Chakravartyji who took him as a disciple and for some 11 years instructed him in the Bengali *Sattvika Tantra* tradition.

Since 1978 Shri Sarvabhavana has been translating the Vedic scriptures from old Bengali and Sanskrit into English. Since just 1969 some 14 volumes of this work – which is between 500 and 5000 years old and which deals with the philosophy of *Bhakti yoga* which has at its core devotion to God and the personal aspect of God – have been published.

Since 1996 Shri Sarvabhavana lives half the year in Berlin and the other half in India. He is still to date engaged in translating and since 2012 as visiting lecturer in Hinduism in the Faculty of Theology of the Humboldt University in Berlin. (International Masters Course, "Religion and Culture").

André Wagner

ARTIST STATEMENT

Ich reise gern ins Unbekannte. An Orte, von denen ich noch nichts weiß. Ich will mich an nichts erinnern können … Wenn ich dort ankomme, will ich nicht an der Oberfläche dahingleiten, sondern mit meiner Kamera das Verborgene, das Unsichtbare sichtbar machen. Dazu musste ich ein Suchender werden ohne Ziel.

2004 reiste ich zum ersten Mal nach Indien, kam gemeinsam mit einem Freund in Neu-Delhi an. Ich war dabei einer Anziehung gefolgt, die ich auch heute noch nicht erklären kann. Ich vertraute einfach darauf, zur richtigen Zeit am richtigen Ort zu sein, um an der „Romance of Elements“, einer Fotoserie zum Thema Feuer, weiterzuarbeiten. Und Indien hat mich wie ein Staubkorn herumgewirbelt, vor sich hergetrieben … und dabei immer wieder zu Boden fallen lassen.

Ich wusste nichts über dieses Land und hatte damals exakt 108 Filme eingepackt. In den vedischen Schriften gilt diese Zahl als heilig. Dabei steht sie für die insgesamt 108 Upanishaden – die vedischen Texte, die die absolute Wahrheit offenbaren. Die 108 ist gleichzeitig eine mystische Zahl – wobei die Zahl 1 für die eine höchste Gottheit steht, die 0 für die Ewigkeit und die 8 für die Zusammenfügung von Gottheit und Ewigkeit. Außerdem steht die 8 auch für die individuelle Seele. Die Quersumme von 108 ist 9 – diese Zahl steht für die Fülle und die Vollkommenheit in der Verwirklichung von Gott und Ewigkeit.

Auf meinen Reisen, immer auf der Suche nach Fotomotiven, bin ich zu Fuß auf Pilgerwegen quer durch Indien gestreift. Ich lernte Pilger kennen, und in gebrochenem Englisch erzählten sie mir von den Göttern der vedischen Religion, die im Alltag der Menschen höchst lebendig sind und ihr Leben seit Jahrtausenden bestimmen. So habe ich Indien durch diese Pilger und durch das Fenster der vedischen Schriften kennengelernt, um es schließlich mit meiner Kamera einzufangen.

Ich lebte wie in einem Rausch, ließ mich ein auf das Fremde, das mir zunehmend besser gefiel, bis es mir schließlich vertraut vorkam. Ich erlebte an diesen heiligen Orten in den Alltäglichkeiten Mitgefühl und Barmherzigkeit. Ganz schlicht.

Ich liebte es, nachts durch die Straßen zu streunen. Nach Sonnenuntergang, wenn die Inder ihr Land durch einen Seitenausgang zu verlassen scheinen … und sich plötzlich Leere offenbart. Tagsüber allein an Leere zu denken erscheint nahezu absurd. Nichts ist bei Tageslicht privat, nichts bleibt unbemerkt … allein die Nächte haben keine Augen.

Die Faszination, die dieses Land und seine Menschen bis heute auf mich ausüben, lässt mich immer wieder nach Indien zurückkehren. Und mit jeder Reise tauche ich tiefer in dieses unvergleichliche, chaotische und widersprüchliche Indien ein.

Meine Arbeitsweise wurde ebenfalls durch die indische Philosophie nachhaltig verändert: Lange Belichtungszeiten transportieren für mich ganz deutlich Vergangenheit, Gegenwart und Zukunft … die hier miteinander verschmelzen.

Das Wissen um den Einfluss der Dualität und der *Gunas* – der drei Energieströmungen, die alles beeinfussen und bestimmen –

André Wagner

ARTIST STATEMENT

I enjoy travelling into the unknown … to places I know nothing about. I want to be able to have no preconceptions. When I arrive there I don't want to glide over the surface, but with my camera to find the hidden, to make the invisible visible. To do so I had to become a searcher without a goal.

I visited India for the first time in 2004, arriving together with a friend in New Delhi. I had been drawn by an attraction which I cannot explain to this day. I relied simply on being in the right place at the right time in order to continue working on the "Romance of Elements", a photographic series about fire. And India swirled me up like a grain of dust, driving me forward … only to let me, time and again, fall to the ground.

I did not know anything about this country at that time and I had packed precisely 108 films. In the Vedic scripture this number is considered sacred. It refers to the total 108 Upanishads – the Vedic scriptures which reveal the absolute truth. The 108 is, at the same time, a mystical number – in that the number 1 stands for the one highest godhead, the 0 for eternity and the 8 for the conjunction of the godhead and eternity. In addition, the 8 stands also for the individual soul. The checksum of 108 is 9 – this number signifies the abundance and the perfection in the realisation of God and eternity.

In my travels, always in the search for photographic motives, I trod along the pilgrim paths that crisscross India. I got to know the pilgrims, and in broken English they told me of the Gods of the Vedic religion which are most present in the everyday lives of the people and which have, for thousands of years, defined their lives. Thus through these pilgrims and through the window of the Vedic scriptures, I came to know India and finally to capture it with my cameras. I lived as if intoxicated, got more involved with this strangeness, which I increasingly warmed to, until it finally seemed to me strangely familiar. I experienced a commonplace empathy and compassion in these holy places. I loved to stray along the roads at night. After sunset when the Indians seem to leave their country by a side exit . . and suddenly the emptiness is revealed. To think of emptiness during the day appears almost absurd. Nothing is private in the daylight; nothing remains unnoticed … only the nights have no eyes.

The fascination which this country and its peoples still have for me causes me to return again and again to India. And with each journey I am immersed more deeply into this incomparable, chaotic and contradictory land. My own approach has been likewise transformed permanently by Indian philosophy. Long exposure has changed past, present and future for me completely … they merge with one another here. Knowledge of how the influence of the duality and the *Gunas* – of the three streams of energy which determine everything – create variety in this world. The *Gunas*, whose dynamic of construction (passion), preservation (virtue) and destruction (ignorance) is assigned, does not only inform how I do things, it also has reordered my access to the world. My first im-

schafft Vielfalt in dieser Welt. Die *Gunas*, denen die Dynamik von Entstehung (Leidenschaft), Erhaltung (Tugend) und Zerstörung (Unwissenheit) zugeordnet sind, prägen nicht nur meine Sicht auf die Dinge, sie haben auch meinen Zugang zur Welt neu geordnet. Mein anfangs von einem Kulturschock geprägter Blick auf diese von der europäischen so verschiedene Gesellschaft hat sich durch Beobachten und Verstehen in große Zuneigung und Respekt gewandelt.

André Wagner wuchs in Burgstädt in der ehemaligen DDR auf und lebt und arbeitet seit 2004 in Berlin. Seine Ausbildung zum Fotografen beendete er im Jahr 2001. In den ersten Jahren dieses Jahrhunderts begann Wagner, eine Art der Fotografie zu entwickeln, die eine faszinierende Kombination aus Landschafts-Fotografie, Performance und technischem Geschick darstellt. Der junge Fotograf geht virtuos mit seiner Kamera um, wobei er die verschiedenen Möglichkeiten des Lichts ausschöpft. Seine malerischen Fotografien werden mithilfe von Langzeitbelichtung und unter Verwendung von verschiedenen Lichtquellen aufgenommen. André Wagner steht in der Tradition von Laszlo Moholy-Nagy und so lenkt er unsere Aufmerksamkeit auf seine visuell poetischen Bilder, mit denen er auf faszinierende Weise die Ebenen seines Selbst auslotet. Das lässt seine Bilder zu Objekten der Kontemplation werden.

Seine Themen reichen von vertrauten Stillleben über Porträts bis hin zu (Stadt-)Landschaften und verweisen oft sehr klar auf seine innere Beteiligung, was politische Themen anbelangt. Seine detailgenau inszenierten Fotografien sind stets authentisch und nicht digital manipuliert.

André Wagner erhielt für seine Arbeiten mehrere Preise, darunter den *Trierenberg Austrian Super Circuit* im Jahr 2008, den *Prize for Photography about Kaunas*/Litauen im Jahr 2007, den *Hasselblad Austrian Super Circuit* im Jahr 2004 und den *Deutschen Jugendfotopreis* im Jahr 2000. Seine Werke sind in privaten und öffentlichen Sammlungen wie der *BVI* (D), der *Delvag/Deutsche Lufthansa AG* (D), des *Grönemeyer Instituts* (D) und der *Vattenfall AG* (D) vertreten. Seit Ende den 1990er-Jahren stellt er seine Arbeiten in Deutschland und international in Galerien, Museen, alternativen Kunsteinrichtungen sowie im öffentlichen Raum aus.

www.andre-wagner.com

pression of this, from a European perspective, so complex society, was characterised by a cultural shock. It has changed by observation and understanding to a feeling of deep affection and respect.

André Wagner grew up in Burgstädt, in the former East Germany, and lives and works in Berlin. He completed his apprenticeship as a photographer in 2001. In the early 2000s, Wagner began making photographs that constitute an intriguing hybrid of landscape photography, performance and technical skill. He investigates the possibilities of lighting situations with all the virtuosity of his camera technique. His artistic photographs are taken using prolonged exposures and a variety of light sources. In the tradition of Laszlo Moholy-Nagy he calls our attention to his visually poetic images, which reflect the levels of his own insights in a fascinating way. It is this that makes his images objects for contemplation.

His subjects range from intimate still-life, through urban landscape to portrait, referring, often explicitly, to his involvement with political issues. Staging photographs in great detail, he creates authentic images that are not digitally manipulated.

André Wagner has won several prizes for his work, including the *Trierenberg Austrian Super Circuit* in 2008, the *Prize for Photography about Kaunas*/Lithuania in 2007, the *Hasselblad Austrian Super Circuit* in 2004 and the *German Youth Photography Prize* in 2000. His works are represented in private and public collections including *BVI* (D), *Delvag/Deutsche Lufthansa AG* (D), *Grönemeyer Institute* (D), *Vattenfall AG* (D) and others. Since the late 1990s, his work has been exhibited in Germany and internationally in galleries, museums, alternative art institutions and public spaces.

www.andre-wagner.com

FOTOGRAFIEN IN LIMITIERTER AUFLAGE
LIMITED EDITION PHOTOGRAPHS

Für den besonders anspruchsvollen Sammler oder Kunstkenner bietet André Wagner eine feine Auswahl von Fotografien in limitierter Auflage. Jedes Werk ist nummeriert und vom Künstler signiert und wird mit einem entsprechenden Echtheitszertifikat geliefert.

For the particularly discriminating collector or art connoisseur André Wagner offers a fine selection of limited edition photographs. Each work is numbered and signed by the artist and comes with a certificate of authenticity.

DANK
ACKNOWLEDGEMENTS

Andy Lim

Andreas Rost

Beate van den Berg

Beisa Grozdanic

Berlind Wagner

Conrad Maess

Daniel Fiskal

Eunkyoung Song

Familie Förster

Jens Hocher

Jürgen Rink

Kriti Gallery, Varanasi – Petra Manefeld und Navneet Raman

Kuvalesaya Zakheim

Marcus Amara Hugk

Mathias Eimann

Michael Schubert

Museum für Fotografie, Berlin – Dr. Ludger Derenthal

Nicole Löser

Nina Rautenberg

Rainer Christian Kurzeder

Renate Wagner

Sacinandana Swami

Shri Sarvabhavana

Sten Böring-Schmidt

Sylvia Puta

Uwe Tietz

Yogendra Gautam

Zoltán Somhegyi

Übersetzung/translation: Harry Houston
Lektorat/copyediting: Martina Klose, Harry Houston
Repro: www.pridat.com
Gestaltung/graphic design: Kurt Liebig
Druck/printing: Himmer AG, Augsburg

Printed in Germany

Hans-Nietsch-Verlag · Am Himmelreich 7 · 79312 Emmendingen · Germany
www.nietsch.de · info@nietsch.de

ISBN 978-3-86264-217-5